NOBODY ASKED

My Memoir

Pamela Brescia

Copyright © 2021 Pamela Brescia

All rights reserved

Some names and identifying details of people described in this book may have been altered to protect their privacy.

No part of this book may be reproduced, or stored in a retrieval system, or transmitted in any form or by any means, electronic, mechanical, photocopying, recording, or otherwise, without express written permission of the publisher.

ISBN: 9798709851207

Cover design by: Alanna Brescia
Library of Congress Control Number: 2018675309
Printed in the United States of America

*I dedicate this book to my angels:
James Dean, Matthew & Jessica
"May you always believe in the good and the things
you cannot see"*

To The Doctor: My Assault

Out in the center of the field,
In the very middle
Far, far away.
Nobody knows it *(but I do)*
There's a big, black, pit.

You might say it's a
                never
                        ending
                                hole.

                                It's big, round
It echoes when you yell in it.
(It echoes forever.)
There's really no end,
So you kind of have to make one.
I never purposely go there,
It was an accident that it even is at all.

Eighteen years since it was formed.

It never gets bigger,
But it is always there.
I don't fear it,
Actually it's there now to remind me,
I learn from it,
I wouldn't be me without it.
It must always be—
So I just live outside it,
Making sure that everything
Outside of it is breathtakingly beautiful...
And then my life goes on.

                                              Looch

Written in 1997 by Pam Brescia

NOBODY ASKED

My Memoir

Pam Brescia

INTRODUCTION

She was never prepared for half of what she went through, but she got through it. She always will.

She is me.

- Author Unknown

    My story takes place many years ago, and yet only over the past three years have I decided to attempt this book - with a lot of help from therapy. The first time I started writing this book, it was deleted. The second attempt ended up lost in computer space - guess I was using the wrong program. Perhaps the third time's the charm?

    I'm not a writer, mind you. I'm just a woman writing from a young woman's memory. It is hard and frustrating enough due to the story itself, but now, because of my previous failed attempts, it is even more frustrating. I've wanted to quit just so I don't have to relive the memories in my head. Add to that the fact I'm getting older and I'm afraid the details in my mind may slip away, although, strangely enough, thus far, they seem to be coming back stronger, clearer and so real, in fact, I can see it happening in my head as I put it on paper. It's crazy how the mind works. We really have no idea do we - at least I sure didn't; but I feel like I know more today.

So again, with this computer in front of me, alone in a room attempting for, what I pray is, the final time writing this book, good or bad, I'm going to finish it. I think that's why over the years I've attempted so many different things and never really saw any of them through. Bad habit I guess I've never been able to break. That's why this time, this book, this story, will be completed. This is not just to prove to myself that I can complete a task, but I need to write this for me. But I mostly want this to be a help to others who have maybe gone through similar tragedies, or any hard times. That itself gives me more reason to finish this. And with this, perhaps my family will gain a better understanding of who I really am.

I can't ignore the urge to finish this book. It's okay if you don't like it, I only ask that you read it. I don't need opinions, though I'm certainly open to them and questions are always welcomed. Before reading this, you only thought you knew me, but after reading this you may understand a little more of who I am and why I am.

You may also find yourself in some of my story, which, if so, I can only hope you see the main message: not only can you survive certain situations, but you can be happy in the end.

It's so dark only the moon lights my vision, even though I don't want to see what is in front of me. This darkness is like no other, it comes with a fear, a kind of terror so chilling, and numbing, it freezes my entire body. I want to keep my eyes closed, but still the moonlight insists that I see. Later, I would learn it was that light that kept me from fading away, to remind me I was still alive. In the end, when the night is over and I do survive, I know the moonlight truly saved my life.

GROWING UP

I'm just a girl like you. I'm just a beautiful misfit.

I always considered myself to be an average girl from an average family. It was just my mom, my dad and my three brothers. My mom was from New Jersey, my dad from Connecticut. I spent most of my childhood bouncing from one state to the other, until we made our permanent move to Florida.

I have nothing but fond memories of my childhood. Coming from a large Italian family, there was always a Pasta Sunday meal where there was no shortage of family, drama, laughter, joy, and of course, food: pounds of pasta, bowls of meatballs, plates of meat including pork chops, sausage, braciole and bread and salad to complete the spread of food. I can still hear my grandmother yelling for her son, my father, from the kitchen, "Jimmy! Come on Jimmy, eat, eat!" The big hit though on Sundays were her two amazing desserts: graham cracker pie and apple turnovers. Everyone looked forward to them and we were all heartbroken when she passed, knowing she wouldn't be here to make them ever again. Thank God my mother learned and perfected Gramma's graham cracker pie so that the tradition could continue to live on. But her turnover recipe, sadly, died with her.

We'd eat dessert and then she'd show me, while in the kitchen alone, just her and I, how to swig milk from the gallon jug. Yup, right out of the fridge. Gross today? Yes, maybe. But giggling and sneaking as we slammed down the milk was a memory that will forever remain special to me. I even taught it to my kids. My gramma really was one of a kind.

It wasn't unusual then for my father to tease the family, but mostly my Aunt Phyllis, my Uncle Joe's wife. He was always pulling pranks on her, maybe because she kept falling for them? His favorite being "Hey Phyllis this pie smells bad, what do you think?" When she went to smell it, he would gently push it into her face. She fell for it over and over. I sure miss my aunt and those fun, silly memories of her with pie on her face.

Being the first born, it was not uncommon for me to get passed around the table, having kisses pressed into my cheeks as a baby. Once I got too big for that, my uncles would pin me to the floor and rub their bearded chins on my cheeks as well as kiss, pinch and squeeze them until they were bright red. Fortunately, after a while, my brothers and cousins were born and were able to take their share of the cheek pinching. Although I am an older woman now, I still think and reminisce about those times. What I wouldn't do today to have my Uncle George squeeze my cheeks and turn them bright red again. My silly loving uncles, always loving me as only they knew how.

> After we finished eating and
> my cheeks made red

from my uncles' beards, the kids would go outside and play in the backyard on the double gliding swing or play for countless hours in the basement making up silly games. Out back we would all sit on the swing and tell silly stories, swing as high as we could and sometimes walk through my gramma's veggie garden. In the basement she had many cool, old items so making up stories was easy - like pretending we were shopping at a store or taking pots and pans and pretending to cook for our pretend family when we played house. We also loved to play with these tiny little collectible ceramic pieces she had on a shelf in her living room. I still have a few to this day.

Gramma kept these little candies upstairs in the kitchen in a little glass bowl by the window. They were striped with pink, brown and white, which I believe was coconut. They were so yummy, we'd sneak them as often as we could! I remember they were my dad's favorites too - he still loves anything coconut. My gramma was my favorite person on Earth at the time. She meant the world to me. Going to her house when family was there were some of my best memories. Between her smile and the way she spoke to me, you could almost feel her love in the air. I soaked in everything she said. We laughed a lot too. Although she was an old school Italian woman, she always had ways to make me laugh. Teasing my grandpa was one of her favorite things. She loved him, I knew that, but would jokingly make fun of his ways to make us both laugh, or would tell me funny stories about all her sons. Now that I think about it, it's probably why my dad and I are such sarcastic people and always trying to make others laugh - the clowns of the family. Those were happy times in my life back then. I'm glad she was gone before all the ugliness fell upon me. I wouldn't have been able to bear to see her so hurt by my life events.

I'm not sure how old I was, maybe around seven, when we moved from New Jersey. Even though I loved my family that lived there, I was so happy to move back to Connecticut, especially because our new home was a quick bike ride to my grandparents' house. I have many fond memories of living in Connecticut on Hall St, but also good memories while living in New Jersey, the birthplace of my nickname, Loochabella. I felt extra special getting that nickname from a good old friend I use to hang out with in Jersey Shore. I spent lots of great summers there as a kid. We stayed at my grandparents - from my mom's side - summer home and fished, went crabbing in the back yard canal, rode bikes, went to the beach there and at night we hung out. One of my favorite cousins, Wayne - yes I loved them all but I had a favorite because of the things he taught me and the life he lived - which I will be writing about in my next book. He lived an amazing life, both good and bad.

I have three brothers and nothing but good memories of them while growing up. We had the usual arguments now and then, like most siblings do, but nothing negative stands out. I always had my own room growing up being the only girl and all which was definitely a perk at times, while my brothers had to share one big room. In Connecticut, we lived in a cute 3-bedroom 2-bath home on a corner lot. My parents' room was downstairs and the other two bedrooms and a bathroom were upstairs. One small room was mine and the other was the big room where my three brothers slept, in three twin beds. A small bathroom was in the hallway between our rooms and a walk-in attic across from that. Our bedroom closets were the ones where when you walked in they got smaller so you eventually had to squat down because you could no longer stand. I also had spiders every night it seemed in my room, which terrified me and still I hate spiders today. I would yell down to my parents most nights and my mom mostly would come up and down those stairs each time to find and destroy the spider. My mom would be amazed how I could spot one out in the dark. I eventually just slept with the lights on, and when that still didn't work, I'd creep into my brothers' room, go over to my brother Jim and beg him to let me stay with him in his twin bed. He'd let me, every time, even though I knew after a while it was a pain. He just knew how scared I was and always just turned on his side and scooted over. I swear my room was part of the attic.

We had a giant apple tree out front in which my brothers and I built a small fort - but really it was just some pieces of wood up in the tree that we could stand on to grab apples in order to throw apple bombs at people on the ground. I remember that a good friend of ours fell out of that tree. He got up and rode his bike home, but his family still sued my parents anyway, crazy. My dad got us a little wooden log cabin to put under the tree. It was tiny but so were we. My mom made us cute blue and white curtains for it. We actually spent a lot of time in that little log cabin and when we got too big for it we put our duck, Squeaky, in it. Yes, my dad let us get a pet duck. He was just a little duckling when we got him and ended up getting real big. When Squeaky got too big for the little log house, one afternoon my dad put us kids and Squeaky into his old, white station wagon and took us to Beach Land Park. Here he put Squeaky in the lake, we said our goodbyes, and we drove away. Hanging out of the back of that old wagon, crying, we watched as Squeaky came out of the water and tried to follow us home, but we were too fast. Or my dad drove off too fast, maybe on purpose. I hope Squeaky lived a nice, long life at that lake.

We had an above ground pool in our yard that we loved and used every summer and a sandbox in the back corner of our house where we eventually buried our turtle. There was also a cherry tree that hung over from the neighbor's yard and we always enjoyed eating the cherries right from the tree. We had, what I thought at the time, a big front and side yard. When it snowed we had amazing snowball fights with the neighborhood kids. Our yard was on a corner lot and surrounded by bushes so it made it more like a fort. We built igloos out of snow to store our snowballs in before the fights started, and we made big, funny looking snowmen too. The winter day I remember most vividly, though, was a morning before I needed to leave for school. I went out in the backyard and licked the metal fence pole. Now, I'm not sure why I did this; maybe to delay going to school? But when I did, my tongue got stuck on that cold, icy fence pole. I was alone, so I felt I had to pull my tongue off and when I did I ended up leaving some of it on the pole. I ran into the house, not really screaming but more moaning for my mom for help with my tongue since it was, at that point, bleeding. I couldn't stop thinking of my piece of tongue out on that pole so, I went back outside with a butter knife and proceeded to scrape my tongue skin with those little holes in it off the metal pole. I wasn't able to get it all off which always made me wonder how long it stayed there. I still wonder to this day, at times, if the remnants are still there.

When I wasn't playing with my friends or with my brothers, I'd ride my bike to my gramma's house. I could also ride to my Uncle Bill's house, which was a block behind my grandparents' house. My younger cousins lived there, and since I was pretty close with all my cousins, it was nice to know they were a bike ride away. Of course, I always had to call first and ask my aunt if it was okay since they were quite a bit younger. But I was always happy when she said yes.

A few times a week after school, and on some weekends, I would ride my bike over to my grandparents' house. I was close with both of them, but I was *really* close with my gramma. It was extra nice for me when it was just the two of us, without all the family around. She and I would do laundry downstairs while my grandpa was out walking or shopping. He couldn't drive so he walked to do everything he needed to. I remember my uncles eventually, as my grandpa got older, put his address on a little piece of paper in his top pocket in case he got lost, which had happened a few times, so he could show the police or whoever to help him get back home. It's so silly, but he seriously walked that many miles away. Maybe that's why he lived to be 91!

I would hang out with my gramma and sometimes even go to work with her when she cleaned hotel rooms part-time at the hotel my Uncle Joe managed. It was fun because some of those times I was allowed to sit at the front desk where the women working there would teach me the switch board as calls came in. Though most days during the week, because she only worked a few days, I would be at her house in the kitchen while she cooked and baked and spoke mostly about God. She would open her bible and read me beautiful verses and teach me to know and love Jesus. She was always so bold and bright and filled with love. I know she had a hard time raising five, very tough boys. She and my grandfather didn't have much and didn't have much of an education, but my gramma taught me how, through God, she had made it through many tough times. The most important lesson she taught me was to always believe what was in my heart to be true and to always be true to myself. Just YOU believing, no need for proof or to prove to others, just you and GOD and what you believe will get you through this life just fine - until heaven calls you home. I guess because it came from her, and all she taught me and showed me about GOD, Jesus and the bible, I just believed. I still believe.

I loved my life in Connecticut with my family close by and around me all the time. However, this ended suddenly around 1974 when my dad announced we were moving to Florida. *What??!! Why??!! Oh my God no one is there that we know. What will we do? It's too hot there. I HATE YOU!!* This is just one of my reactions I had as a teen when I heard this news. Dramatic, yes, but geez why would he do this to me, to our family?! I was going to die, ugh. Life was over, or so I thought at that point. But, obviously, life continued on, and Florida eventually became home.

As you can imagine saying goodbye to my family and the few friends I had, my misfits, was pretty hard at my age and very emotional. I knew I'd have to start at a new school, a middle school no less, and that was a really scary thought. We had to stay at a hotel for a short time while the house we would be renting was being prepared for our arrival. The house was in a small, up and coming neighborhood, part of Pompano Beach, so things were really new. Our home was a nice

4-bedroom 2-bath house with a small fenced-in yard in a pretty neighborhood where most of the homes looked the same with only slight differences in the color, room setup or whether or not there was a pool. I quickly learned that there were many other new families with kids my age and more moving in, which somehow made it seem easier. Once I was signed up and school had started, I could figure out which kids lived near me. It turned out many students lived in my neighborhood, which was awesome and meant that I would have people to hang out with after school.

SCHOOLING

I like weird people. The black sheep. The eight balls. The left centers. The wallflowers. The underdogs. The loners. The rejects. The outcasts. The outsiders. The odd ducks. The eccentric. The broken. The lonely. The lost and forgotten. The misfits. These are my people.
- Author unknown

    I started elementary school in Connecticut. I don't remember being as excited as other children may have been, and for a few reasons. One being I had to go first before my 3 younger brothers, kind of like a test dummy, to see how scary it really was, I suppose and more so because I really was okay being home with my family. It just felt safe. But it's what I had to do, so off I went. Hello kindergarten.

    I don't remember much in the beginning, I mean it started out okay, but as I got older, around 10 or so, I started getting teased. They called it being teased back then, but to me it felt like bullying. I got teased mostly about my frizzy hair, crazy when I think of it today, but it was a lot and constant and I left school crying often. It became a part of my school day and it eventually led me to distance myself from others. I didn't know how to respond or fight back, so I did my best to just deal with it. I remember one incident while sitting on the bleachers at a game. The girls behind me started pulling and yanking on my braids - I wore braids often because of how thick my hair was- so I turned around, gave them my mean face and yelled at them to stop. One of the girls thought it would be funny to light the ends of my hair on fire, she must have had a lighter with her, because she actually lit the ends! I put it out quickly, obviously, but what's even crazier is that I didn't do anything or tell anyone about how I was being treated. Soon after they began calling me Brillo head - a name that stuck all the way through middle school.

I came to hate school, everything about it. I learned to dislike certain groups of people and hated all my teachers for never noticing my pain, or even me for that matter. The bullying taught me that mean people sucked and that I couldn't do anything to fight them. I decided I would start hanging out with, what I considered then, the cool kids, the misfits. Misfit, to me, meant people that didn't fit into what others called a "normal" group, people like myself that got picked on: people that cared more about things like music, the Earth and how they treated other people rather than cheerleading or dating football stars, or who's wearing what or dating who. I found those kinds of people, those misfits, and I became lost to the mean people. I became unnoticed, almost invisible to them. But even better than that, I was

noticed by the small group of friends that I had started to make - the other misfits.

I can't say I remember having a best friend then. I played with the girls in my neighborhood and my brothers' friends in the yard, but I didn't have a friend that I could confide in, which was just fine. As I got a little older, things became a little easier at school. Being invisible was not so bad, though I still hated school. It was when I was not in school, though, that I had the most fun just being with my family and the few kids I knew.

I was not a good student in school, especially high school. After experiencing the party life not long after moving to Florida, I never wanted to be another brick in the wall at school. I was stoned most times, morning till night, including during school. Whenever I got a chance to smoke in the parking lot, the hallways, the bathrooms, I took it. I skipped as much as possible to avoid being in class, which usually meant I had to do summer school every summer just to keep up. I knew only a few people in high school and most of them were from my neighborhood, though I did hang out with a few other misfits like myself that weren't from my neighborhood. But since my boyfriend didn't go to the same school as me, I would usually stay home after school to be with him. Being a misfit then, and today as well, was a good thing. I didn't want to be like any of the other girls or part of their cliques. I guess it was the punk in me, the rebel, thinking I had to fight to be different, when in fact, it came naturally.

There were many cliques at school, most of which I hated and avoided as much as possible. It was always hard for me to fit in because of the 'misfit' title I gave myself and because I didn't *really* want to fit in. I didn't care about cheerleading or after school events or sports. I didn't care about the cute boys liking me or even knowing who I was - no prom or dances for me. I just went because I had to and I found my own ways of getting through it all. I made a few friends in my neighborhood that became good friends after a while. In school we didn't see or hang out with each other much except for when we would leave a class and head to the beach, but definitely more after school. During that time I started smoking cigarettes which quickly led to *everything* else. One thing my friends and I had in common was getting high and drinking. After school and after dinner we would all meet up on the corner of our block, sit on the concrete curb or the electrical boxes between our homes and just hang out, talk, laugh, get high, sip on some Mad Dog 20/20 and eventually, some of us would fool around, but just a little, though some more than others.

I remember one girl in particular, Kathy, I met in high school; she had a big impact on my life. Both of her parents had passed away and she was living with her brother. She faced many challenges growing up without her parents and felt alone, especially in high school. We were both lonely people who found each other and helped each other not feel so alone in the world.

She was private and to herself, like me at the time. I felt at home around her and she made going to high school a bit more bearable. After we started hanging out for awhile, I brought her to my house to meet my family, which she thought was amazing since she really did not have one. We hung out in my room or walked to the local stores to get smokes or just hung out and met people along the way. Back then, Janis Joplin and her music meant a lot to the both of us. Her music and words would give us such pleasure, we felt free and, in a way, special. We would play and sing one song in particular over and over again on my stereo, pretending we had mics in our hand as we blasted out the words. She and I had a very special line from Joplin's *Piece of my Heart*. We would send it in notes to each other, or say it just when we were feeling good. In those moments, Kathy reminded me so much of Joplin - her crazy brown hair flinging around her face, her hippy like qualities, but most of all her free spirit. I loved her in the most beautiful, loving way. So, when she eventually moved away it was super hard on me because she would have been the one person I could have told about that tragic night. She was the person I could have sat with for hours, even days, talking to; someone who I could have confided in, someone who could have understood my pain and helped me through it, who cared. But, it happened after she left. We tried to stay in touch and did so for many years, writing letters and calling. But, as we all know, time has a way of separating us from those we love and we just have to move on with our lives. The letters stopped. I lost her. I haven't had a friend like her since.

When we lost contact in the late seventies, I never thought I would get back in touch with her, but thanks to social media, we were able to reconnect in 2012. I called the university I found out she was working at in Gainesville and asked if they knew Kathy M. and what department she was in. To my surprise, they connected me to her. I couldn't believe she picked up the phone. I asked if she was Kathy M, and she said "Yes. How can I help you?" I then recited our favorite line from the Joplin song we both loved as teenagers. "Pam?" she said. We spoke and cried for an hour that day and tried to plan visits over the next few years. In 2014 I saw on her Facebook page that Kathy had suddenly passed away. She was 53 years old and loved by so many at the university that she worked at. I struggled with the fact that I had lost such a beautiful friend, but I also struggled with the fact that we never got to meet or visit before her death. I should have just driven to Gainesville, but I didn't.

When we were younger we didn't allow life to get in our way, but as we got older, we did. I think she knew she was ill which is why she would always come up with an excuse when we talked about meeting up. Although it hurts to know we didn't get to see each other again, I will always be grateful that I got to speak to her before she died. I learned an important lesson from this - don't lose contact with people you love, make time for them. My life could be completely different if she were still here, but now I'll never know, and that's okay. Kathy was a beautiful soul who was taken too soon, and will be remembered by me forever.

FIRST LOVE

Flowers grow back, even after they are stepped on. So will I.

-Charles Eriksson

When we moved to Florida, to the new rental house, I had my own bedroom that was, thankfully, spider free. My brother Jim got his own room while Rob and Scott shared one. We were still close, but by then we were all pretty much in our teens, except Scott, the youngest, and all into our own things. When we did see each other, which wasn't as often due to school, after school activities, homework, etc., it was at family get togethers or family dinners at home or sometimes in front of the tv. The oldest of us would sometimes end up in the same group of friends, which was pretty cool, but generally we had our own groups we hung out with, our own music we liked, our own ways of partying, our own ways of getting through life. I loved and still love *all* 3 of my brothers. Even with all our differences, even with all the crazy times we went through, even though we didn't hang out all the time, I knew they were always there. I really believe we had a pretty good childhood and I'm grateful. Looking back, it seems my childhood went by so fast, too fast in fact. I wish I could have slowed it down, hung out with them a little more, but I guess that's what life teaches you - to spend the time with those you love when you have the opportunity. Fortunately, as we grew into adults, we became closer and remain very close to this day. Each of my brothers are important and special to me in their own ways. I can't imagine my life without them.

My parents always taught us that family comes first. You stick by your parents, right or wrong, and that you be there for your brothers and sister, no matter what. Familia first, is what we were taught! They instilled this in us by example and we lived by it as best we could when we were young. Even today we teach our own children the same. But as you will find out, I didn't share everything.

My brother Jim had a few cool friends and I became attracted to one in particular. But at 13 or 14 years old that meant someone to be by your side, hang out with, fool around with, but not necessarily have sex with them. I was still a virgin at this point, but that changed around the time I was 15 years old and met, who I thought at the time, the love of my life. My brother's friend lived in two different places - one up north with his mom's family and with his dad's family in Florida. He was a bit of a rebel, a troublemaker, and a real asshole at times; he wasn't well liked by many, but for some unknown reason, the moment I laid eyes on him, I was attracted to him and wanted to get to know him. And I made sure that I did.

One night, while hanging with some friends and my brother in front of our house, a taxi pulled up. The door opened and out he walked, with a huge smile and booming voice, "Hey what's up?" My eyes met with his, and it was all over for me. I didn't know how to act. I had never felt this way about anyone, not even my first boyfriend. All I knew was that I wanted to kiss this guy. I imagined he was there to see me, not my brother, and that he would walk up to me, put his arms around me and kiss me hello. Of course, that was just a silly daydream, because all I got as he walked right past me, was a "Hey! How's it going?" and he went off with my brother and the girls they hung out with. Oh well.

Eventually over time I fell deeply in love with this young, troubled rebel friend of my brother's. I didn't care what other people thought about him. There was a connection I could not ignore and he was the first boyfriend I had that I loved. I was 15 years old and in love. I kind of liked the fact that he was a rebel, a tough guy. I'm not sure why, but I liked the fact that he cried when we were alone, that he could express his pain and tell me his story. He had a very troubled past, but I didn't care. I loved being with him and wanted to be around him as much as I could. I even took him back many times after he would go to be with other girls or be missing for days while partying with his guy friends. It didn't matter - I loved him.

I had heard from other girls about their first time having sex. Their experiences were ugly, hurtful, they felt used and had pain. My first time was quite different. My first time with this man I loved was magical, a moment I loved and will never forget. I remember it was at my cousin's apartment. We had snuck into one of the bedrooms and locked the door while others were out in the living room. It seemed so exciting at the time. Through the years I learned many things from this lover. He taught me so much about sex that no one had talked to me about, ever. People eventually found out we were a couple, and I don't think that went over too well, but we didn't care. We had fun hanging out with the friends that liked being around us - going to concerts, parties, hitchhiking around, hanging out at the beach, skipping school and having lots of laughs. But, as time went on, I pretended not to notice the ugly in our relationship, the things others made comments about. Perhaps it's that I didn't know any better, or maybe it's just that I didn't want to face it, but there were signs that I now know are not okay in a true, loving relationship - signs that eventually caused the end of this one.

I was constantly accused of cheating and it didn't matter who I was with or what I was doing. To him, I was cheating on him with everyone and anyone - his brother, his best friends, a neighbor, a stranger. At first I thought it was cute because he loved me and it was like a confirmation that he didn't want me to be with anyone else, just him. I eventually made excuses when others noticed his jealousy, always defending it, "he's just a jealous guy, I think it's cute." But as I got older, and many years later, I learned that jealousy is *NOT* part of love. Trust is. Trusting each other 100%, no questions asked. This was not part of our relationship. If he only knew the truth today, that I never did cheat on him, not once, perhaps he would have appreciated me more then and learned more for his future relationships.

I remember the first time the jealousy turned physical. We were at one of his family functions up north, where he was from, and all the young adults had stayed up drinking, playing cards and talking. It was my first visit to his mom's home and I had just met most of them and was having a good time, laughing, drinking and getting to know his family and friends. At one point I looked over at him, as he was sitting across from me, and I noticed his face getting more serious - no more laughing or smiles. I could feel his mood change, and I was right. He asked me to come out front for a smoke so we could talk. I thought that was strange since it was freezing outside, being the middle of December and all, but we put on our coats and sat out front on the cold concrete steps. He stood up from the stoop and immediately asked "What the hell are you doing? Why are you in there flirting with all those other guys?" He was accusing me of flirting with the men at the table?! I couldn't believe it. I responded to him, "what are you talking about?" Before I knew what happened, he had backhanded me across my mouth. I was shocked. I'd never been hit by anyone, not another girl in a fight, not even by my own father. I was stunned. I put my hand to my lip and felt warm blood instantly turn cold in the winter air. There wasn't a lot of blood and it didn't hurt exactly; I was more shocked that someone who claimed they loved me just smacked me. I didn't say anything. I just looked at the blood on my fingers then back at him. Perhaps he really was sorry that time, as he dropped down to his knees and started to apologize over and over again, "I can't believe I did that. Oh my god baby, I'm so sorry. Forgive me, I hate myself." There I was, alone there with his family, out of my element and far from my own family, so I forgave him. I really thought he was sorry, but over the years the more abuse I endured the word 'sorry' was accompanied with tears. It made it easier to forgive that way, and I kept forgiving.

Obviously I'm an adult now, and know that his jealousy was his own insecurity and had nothing to do with me. There were countless times that I was spit on, directly in my face, kicked while down, grabbed and twisted till there were small bruises on my arms and legs, headaches from my hair being pulled, clothes cut up, furniture thrown, sometimes out the front door. Holes in the walls became common and I patched them up as fast as they appeared.

He was always careful, probably from fear of my family finding out, not to hit me in the face or leave marks that could be seen - those I could not hide.

Yes, I was definitely part of the hiding and lying - he couldn't do it alone. It takes two as they say. Each time he was more sorry than the last, each time my fault, always my fault somehow.

I certainly wasn't perfect and I'm sure I pissed him off at times. Couples argue, couples disagree, but never was it acceptable for me to be abused like that. Never did I deserve to be degraded in so many ways or have his *loving* hands on me in that manner. The verbal abuse, the mean, hurtful words did just as much damage to me as the physical. The physical eventually healed, but the pain from his words burned into my brain forever. To think all that while we were dating.

We broke up a lot in between dating and marrying, mostly due to him disappearing and reappearing with a new girl while we were broken up. We somehow always got back together. I always took him back. I always forgave him. I loved him. I knew the pain from his upbringing so I made excuses and thought I could help him, change him, teach him. As time went on and we dated more seriously, I eventually started losing friendships, seeing family less and less, changing the way I dressed, not listening to the same music, slowly losing myself, all to keep what I thought was the peace in my home. I forgave him again and again, over and over. I'd convinced myself and others he could do no wrong, it wasn't his fault, even though I knew it was in many ways.

We not only continued dating but eventually married and started a family. How silly we were to think marriage would do anything to make this situation better, but like I said earlier, when it was good, it was really good. I did love him. Today I think, how dare we do that to innocent children. I mean how dare we put them in a home where there was so much hiding and hurt. What selfish human beings we were. So much turbulence before marriage, why didn't we just wait. Kids don't make a bad situation better, marriage doesn't calm them down or make those serious issues go away. How silly to think that love is putting your hands, in anger, on people you claim to love or hurting them with damaging, insulting, abusive words.

By age 21 we were married with our first child on the way and I did everything to protect that child, or so I thought. I thought that by keeping a smile on my face everyday was protecting him; I thought that by staying married to his father was protecting him; I thought hiding in the bathroom or in the bedrooms singing *Jesus Loves Me*, was protecting him. I thought all those marriage counselors we saw over the years would help - I really tried, we both tried. Eventually we had two more children which now made three, and literally all of them made the ugly parts of my life seem so right, so beautiful! Suddenly I was a mom and I learned a whole new type of love having the three of them, and the best part of my life was having them in it. I learned how to smile even when times were rough. They had no idea of the ugly that went on, not when they were little, I made sure. Our children were, and still are, the greatest things in our lives. They are the best thing we ever created together and were most definitely created out of pure love, because none of the ugly had anything, at all, to do with them.

Their dad and I did love each other the only way we knew how at the time. To this day, my children are the greatest parts of my life. I'm sorry to all three of them for any and all of my choices and mistakes that may have hurt them along the way because no parent ever purposely tries to hurt their child. We just do our best, or what we think is our best at the time, and learn along the way. Sadly, what's done is done and there's so much I wish I could take back. These aren't necessarily regrets, just changes I would make; however, I can't and in many ways that's okay too. If I were able to change the past, who knows where I'd be today. Perhaps my precious children wouldn't be here and that wouldn't make sense to my life at all. If I can speak up now and hopefully help the next generation or someone who may be going through a similar situation, it will all be worth it, that's what's most important today.

I feel like these early signs need to be pointed out even though they may be difficult for some to see and read. For some that know and choose to ignore the signs as I did then, and for some of us to face the truth yet still choose to ignore, I feel this is important to bring to light. Sometimes when we are young and in love, or what we believe is love, we get lost and lose ourselves just to be loved. A lot of times this happens even when we are not so young. Sadly, I see it today in many adults that just want someone there with them, so they settle for good enough.

We convince ourselves that this love is

different from all the rest and that it doesn't matter where we come from, or how much love we come from, this boyfriend/spousal love is a different love. It's not part of a family type of love, this love is our very own.

One of the first and ugliest warning signs is jealousy - it's also the easiest to dismiss, like it's common or not a big deal. It can sneak into your relationship without notice, causing small innocent questions to become bigger, more damaging ones as time goes on; and, before long, a huge issue. Another is not knowing how to compromise. So we, as young women, just give in and allow the man to take more control, and make more decisions just not to argue or upset him. Over time the deeper we get into our relationship the easier it is to not see a way out of all the issues that follow. For many it is just easier to keep the peace and make excuses thinking we're trying to make it work, when in fact we are either scared to get out or think it will change....so the years pass by, until we find our light.

THE NIGHT THAT CHANGED MY LIFE

I am not what happened to me. I am what I choose to become.

-Carl Jung

It started out like any other night - hanging out with some friends for a while, then going home. I went home a little early that night; there wasn't much to do. My parents weren't home when I got there, I think they went to dinner with some friends, which was pretty common. Soon after getting home, I got a call from a girl named Shari. Shari was a friend of a friend and I was starting to hang out with her a little more. She was a misfit like me. We got high together, got lunch, went to the mall, and sometimes we went to each other's houses to hang out. But mainly we got high together. Shari lived with her mom and mom's girlfriend. I always saw this as normal, but back then, to the rest of the world, it was not. I never knew where her father was and she had no siblings, so I knew how important friends were to her. Of course she got teased by others for her parents' choices, which contributed to her being labeled a misfit.

On this particular night, she called and asked if I had any weed. I didn't, so she asked if I could get a car to pick her up so we could go get some. I figured since my parents weren't home and they did have two cars, I'd borrow the one. I told her sure and that I'd be right over, not knowing of course that this night would be different from all the rest. That this night would change my life forever.

It was evening when I left to pick up Shari. Truth is, to this day, I am still not sure of the dates, times and how long I was gone that night, just that it was summer and evening. Strangely, those specific details didn't stick in my memory, only the really ugly ones.

I beeped the horn and Shari came out, smiling. Happy to see me, or perhaps happy that she found a ride to go get weed, I will never know. Either way, she was smiling. She hopped in the front seat and off we went. She lived in a city close to mine and where we were going was closer to Pompano. While driving in my parents' car Shari and I talked a little, but not about anything that sticks out. As I went down the road past the Day Inns I saw the Strip club ahead and was about to make my turn into the neighborhood where we purchased our weed, when suddenly and very clearly, I heard a loud *NO!* It was a deep, loud, clear, almost echoing, very serious *NO!*

Frightened, I hit the brakes, looked over at Shari and said, "did you hear that?" This occurrence startled me because, although I'd had visions as they were happening and had visits from loved ones that had passed on, this one seemed to be loud and distinct. Perhaps it was because I was not yet grown up and not aware of who I was at that point. I would usually ignore it, thinking it coincidence or tell myself it didn't really happen, but the loud warning of *NO* that night felt real and I knew I shouldn't have ignored it.

"Tell me you heard that!" I pressed Shari again.

"No! No, I didn't hear anything. What the hell are you talking about?" she asked with confusion.

"I'm sorry." I said. "I thought I heard something; never mind." Ignoring those instincts again, my foot went from the brake to the gas pedal and we slowly entered the neighborhood as the evening continued to fall into darkness.

It was in an area where us kids would go to buy nickel-and-dime bags in a lower income neighborhood; a neighborhood well-known for quickly grabbing a nickel-and-dime bag of weed, like a drive through bank or an In-and-Out fast food burger joint. I knew all the precautions because my friends and I frequented this area many times before. But this time I felt unsure for some reason. We were two, young, white girls going in alone. On the way I reminded Shari to keep the doors locked, remove all jewelry and to only open the window long enough to slip the money out and the
nickel-and-dime bag in. Boom. Just like that it was usually a done deal - but not this time, not this night.

My dad's car was a 4-door that had automatic locks, which of course I made sure were locked before driving on. I drove a little ways into the neighborhood until I saw a small group of guys on the corner. I pulled up, as I have many times before, took the $5 dollars from Shari and folded it up to fit out the crack of the window. I let them know I only wanted one baggie, and put the $5 out the crack of the window and pulled my baggie into the car. That was it, how it always went - money out, drugs in. I knew never to put the car in park but to always keep it in drive so that when I made the deal I could put my foot back on the gas pedal. Before I had the chance to put my foot on the gas, I heard the doors unlock. The two back doors and passenger door opened and I immediately felt a cold metal object connect with the back of my head. Did it come from the back seat? I was frozen with fear and confusion. The next few moments of this nightmare would change my life forever. The person I was would forever be gone and a different version of myself would emerge. The nightmare had only begun.

"Drive, bitch! Drive!" someone with a loud, deep voice yelled over and over. The deep voice echoed and vibrated in my ears along with other voices. The only sound coming from Shari and I were our cries. Oh my god! What was happening? The yelling, demanding voices made my head hurt and filled it with too much confusion. I drove, or did I? Was this real? How did I know where to drive? My mind was working, trying to understand what was happening. Where was Shari? She was sitting in the front seat next to me. Who was next to me now? I was too scared to look anywhere but in front of me. Who was in the back? Everything was unknown, so unreal. I knew I was going to die, that I was driving to my death. I wanted my mom, my dad, my family. I was even more terrified when I realized the cold metal against my head was actually a gun. Something was happening to my mind at that point. It was leaving my body. It was like my mind and body were no longer one, no longer connected, but somehow separated. So, like a robot, disconnected, I followed the directions that were barked at me and kept my foot on the gas pedal, not knowing where I was driving.

It seemed to be darker, even though I had no idea of the time. I felt like I was driving further and further into the night, but I was sure it had only been minutes. We turned up and down a few streets and then turned at a corner and went off the street onto a dirt road that led to a canal. It was there I was told to stop and shut the car off. I did and someone immediately swiped the keys from the ignition. I never saw those keys again. I heard all the doors open and a man's voice yell loudly, "Get out! Get out! Come on over here!" I still don't know how many people were there. I still don't know where Shari was. I just felt that hard metal gun now being pressed into my upper back as someone pushed me towards the canal. Near the dirt road there was a bit of dead grass, an old piece of plywood and some trash laying around all in the grass close to the water. My mind quickly started wandering through varying crazy thoughts, but nothing came out of my mouth. My mind spoke to, who I now know today, was God. *Oh God he's going to shoot me and throw my body into the canal. I can't believe I'm going to die right now, right here tonight and my body thrown in a canal - so near my home. Who's going to find my body? A stranger the next day? Maybe a few days since I'm kind of hidden here or maybe my body will float down the canal behind someone's home? I wonder who will find me first, maybe a cop? Or what if a child sees me? Will they tell? How long will it take for anyone to know I'm even missing? My friends and family will probably think I was just out partying. Jesus! My parents will be so broken when they get the news.* I couldn't imagine the pain they'd endure. I was so scared. *Please, God, I can't die like this. I haven't even lived yet. I'm in love with this boy, and God I have to finish high school. I graduate next year. I need to get my dad's car back soon or he'll be so disappointed in me. Please not tonight, not like this.* I continued walking like a robot towards the canal and thought to myself, *how do I even prepare to die? I don't know how to do this! I guess I will hear the intense scream from the gun and then I'll know. After that nothing will matter.* So I just kept slowly walking forward because I had absolutely no other choice.

I was roughly pushed down onto the piece of plywood near the dead grass by the canal at the end of the dirt road. Laying on my back I looked up at the night sky and saw nothing, nothing but darkness. It was scary because everything was dark and black around me. I kept my eyes tightly closed, then suddenly felt the heaviness of a body on me and a man entering me. I knew instantly I was being raped. It's hard to explain the actual feeling of what it's like to be raped, but you just know. It's like I knew by the darkness, the fear, the place and the utter coldness that someone was having sex without me giving permission, and I felt like I could vomit. It's a cold disgusting feeling that runs through your entire body, nothing like having sex. It's like someone pumping ice cold fluids into your veins, a chill I could feel throughout my body, a deep sickening feeling. I believed it should have hurt physically; in fact it should have been so painful that I screamed out, but I didn't. I felt almost nothing, no real physical pain then. I think my mind retreated to a place that protected me in a way. Like the child that is being abused - they go to a place in their minds, not on purpose, that protects them in ways, takes them out of the place they are and brings them to safety almost. I can imagine a prostitute doing something like this, though her choice, but while with her Johns, finding a way to not be there so she can get through what she believes she must.

I took myself out of my physical body and floated above, just gone. I knew what was happening, just not feeling the pain from it. I knew I was being raped and started wondering what was next. Would I be murdered? That's how these things usually go, right? I can't be let go because I saw the faces of the criminals so I must be killed. I didn't let myself feel the physical slaughter that was happening, but the psychological side of what was happening to me was terrifying. He stopped after a minute and had me remove a tampon that I didn't even realize was there. Like a robot, I did so. When I leaned up to remove it I looked over and saw a small group of men and Shari sitting on the hood of my dad's car, smoking. My mind was blurry and my sight seemed cloudy, but I saw what I saw. I was pushed back down onto my back. I looked up at the dark sky for just a moment before I again closed my eyes tightly, while being raped continuously. My mind wandered off. *Why did it seem like that group of people were just hang-*

ing out, talking and smoking while, just a few feet away, I'm being raped? Why didn't Shari scream? Why wasn't she being raped, or was she already? These thoughts helped me to not feel so much of what was happening, but my mind wanted to explode. I turned my head to the west and got a glimpse of the moonlight. I wanted to keep looking at it, but I was afraid it would show my assailant's face. I had no idea how long I was on that board when it suddenly stopped.

I was told to get up. The gun was in his hand, so I listened. The next thing I knew I was back in my dad's car but not as the driver. I was in-between two men in the front seat, again, unsure of who was in the back and where Shari was. I felt even scarier now having no control of the car and knowing it was in the hands of someone scary and dangerous. In a crazy way, and for just a second, I thought maybe they were going to drop us off on the main road and take the car, but that was the furthest thing from their plan. The driver drove my dad's car all through the neighborhood. I remember how dark it was. I remember thinking to myself *I'm alive, but where am I? Will I be living in someone's home forever as a prisoner? Will they drive to another city or state?* The highway was so close it could happen. Anything could have happened at that point. I went away in my mind again, the same explosion happened in my head and my vision became blurry as I felt the car come to a stop. *Oh my God, now what? Where were we?* I was hurt, tired, but they opened the door and pushed me out of the car. I was led with the gun to my back to what looked like a small baseball field. I also saw what looked like people, shadows of people, but it looked to me like big dark, very scary shadows of monsters. I was pushed the entire way to the field, over to the beginning of the bleachers and then pushed down onto the cold metal. It was loud in my head, besides the ringing from my head hitting the metal benches, I heard men laughing, talking that sounded like mumbling, some louder than others, but nothing I could understand.

In the car was so loud, and by the canal too, but now it seemed even louder, all the sounds became static and I couldn't make out where it was actually coming from. I knew I was on the bottom bleacher because I felt my feet touch the ground. Someone removed my pants and pushed me back onto the metal. With my head on the cold bleacher, I again looked up at the sky. But this time, I didn't close my eyes, not tightly, not at all. My eyes found the moon, a big, full bright moon. The glare from it was hypnotizing, drawing my mind in. It seemed to be calling me to it, making me stare at it, helping me to feel okay. It seemed it was letting me know it was with me and wasn't going to leave me alone. I remember almost feeling warmth from its light on my face.

I felt the same disgusting thrusting and knew the attack on my body was commencing. For a quick moment, with the glow from the moon, I looked behind the man now abusing my body and couldn't believe what I saw - men all around me, lined up, waiting their turn to abuse my body, destroy me, kill my soul, maybe to kill me.

It was night so I couldn't, nor wanted, to see their faces, but I took that quick glance because, in a way, it let me know I was still alive, for my mind was unsure at times. It looked like I was in a movie, but the cold metal bench and the aching in my back sometimes reminded me how real it all was. I liked it better when my mind disappeared and I didn't feel. I looked back to the moon and I knew it was God, I just knew it, so I prayed. I spoke to God the entire time. *God. I know this is not your doing, just evilness on this Earth, but God could you please continue to stay with me? Oh, and thank you for sending the moonlight, it helps so much. Please God, I just want to go home now. I want my mom and dad really bad. I don't feel so good. I feel so alone and sick. Really sick. These men won't stop and God I need them to please just stop. God help me and make them stop, leave my body alone. I just want to go home. I'll be good I promise. Please, please make this stop.*

As the destruction of my body continued and men took turns with me I continued staring up at the moon, praying, talking to God. I have no idea how long, when suddenly, like in a movie, I saw my life quickly flash before me. It was strange and hard to describe, but it was like a short quick film. I saw my parents and my brothers, my house on Hall street in Connecticut where I grew up. I saw faces and places in my head like an old movie reel. Somehow, I'm not sure because I wasn't sure of anything, it seemed that this film, in this moment, took me away from feeling what was actually happening to my body, like what you hear when people meditate into a deep state - their bodies are physically there but they are away off in their minds on adventures. I later learned to meditate, but at that moment, for some unexplained reason, I was able to do so without ever learning and grateful I could. It's like when women are giving birth, they are taught to concentrate on their breathing or look at a spot on the ceiling so that you won't feel as much pain going on in their bodies. My spot on the ceiling was the moon in the sky. So I continued to trust and speak to God that night so I felt close to him, so much safer knowing he was with me. I felt like the moon he sent me was like a speaker that connected directly to his ears, like having his private cell number; call me when you need me. I'll be right here, I've always been. So I seriously asked, *God if there's anything you can do, please God make this stop, I just wanna go home now, please. I promise I'll be good, I'll be better. God I don't see a way out of here on my own. I need you to guide me, show me the way. Please, a sign. I don't think I can stay here much longer. I think I'm just going to die. Is that what's supposed to happen? I mean, if so, I'm ready. I'll go with you. Just make this stop.* I prayed and prayed and begged and begged for what seemed like hours. My body was numb, like I only had a mind, and a weak one at that, no physical body at all.

Out of nowhere, somewhere in the darkness, I heard a woman's voice, "You all get away from that girl! You hear me? Get your asses away from her now! I called the cops!" She screamed over and over, louder and louder, until I felt some pressure release from my chest and heard the men scatter as they cussed at the woman. I slowly turned my head to the right and saw a shadow of a woman who I thought was swinging either a baseball bat or a broom coming towards me as she continued to scream and yell. I felt her grab my right hand. I can still remember how soft and warm her skin felt. I managed to sit my limp, hurt, tired body upright and pull my hand away from hers to feel around for my pants. I don't know if I had panties too, but later learned I didn't. She yelled for me again to get up and come on, that I needed to get out of there. I knew I needed to get out of there, I just didn't know how, so I followed her.

Still feeling like a robot, a human without a brain that could not think on its own, she pulled me over to a small car. In the passenger seat there was a man who, when I approached, opened the door and moved his seat forward so I could get in the back. I stuck my head in first, and there in the back seat was Shari. Confused, I got in, but we didn't speak; we were like strangers. The only person that continued to talk was the woman driver, but
I only heard pieces, until she sternly and loudly said,

"Do you hear me? You got to get the fuck out of here. You got to go. Listen to me! I'm bringing you to a phone booth here. I'm trying to help you, you understand?"

I didn't understand and I felt so trapped in the back seat of that car. I didn't trust her, I didn't trust anything. I couldn't see the moon and felt I'd never get home. Without the moon I felt more lost and alone. I had no idea where I was, if I was even in the same neighborhood. Nothing felt real. I was a zombie now, no longer a robot.

The small car stopped in front of what appeared to be a small convenience store. It was dark in and around the store, like it was closed for the night, or possibly forever. I saw, from what little light her car's headlights produced, a metal phone booth hanging on the outside wall of the building. The car lights went off and the woman yelled, "let her out!" The man in the passenger seat jumped out and moved his seat forward. I made my way out and was so close to him, I wondered for a second if he was one of my rapists, but quickly realized it didn't matter. "Girl hurry up! Go on, call for help now!" the driver shouted to me. I didn't run or panic, but like a dead zombie, I walked over to the phone which I noticed was coin operated - I had no money. I didn't know how to use it or even who to call, but I lifted the receiver thinking maybe an operator would be waiting for my call.

As soon as I put the receiver to my ear, out of nowhere, I heard and felt a BOOM, a loud vibrating explosion, horribly scary sound. I thought it was a bomb. My brain shook, the phone in my hand dropped, the metal booth seemed to vibrate - the sound was deafening. I thought I had literally gone deaf. Everything seemed to echo for so long in my ears and my head was vibrating - all I heard was this high pitch screeching sound ringing in my ears. I looked over at the small car and saw the woman driver waving to me and frantically gesturing to me to get back in the car. I'm not sure why I trusted her, still not thinking clearly I suppose, but I did and moved a bit faster this time. As my senses started kicking in I realized the bomb wasn't a bomb, but a bullet aimed right at me. The bullet, luckily, hit the metal around the phone booth, just missing my head. Shari, when I got back into the car, spoke for the first time in a long while and confirmed what I thought "Oh my God Pam, that was a bullet you know! I saw the spark hit so close to your head!" She sounded so scared, I almost forgot what her voice sounded like at all. I didn't really care about her or the bullet. I just didn't care about anything other than going home. As the woman started driving again I heard all three

voices talking but I didn't, I couldn't even make out what they were all saying. I felt myself start to fade, giving up, really starting to believe more and more that this night just wasn't going to end and if it did it wouldn't end well. I didn't feel any safer being in the car, even though the woman seemed like my rescue. A part of me
knew God was in control, but I didn't know or understand his plan so giving up started to really kick in. I didn't care at this point what would happen either way, dying might be a better option now; perhaps it's where
God thinks I need to be. We drove, and as we approached the outside of whatever neighborhood we were in, I saw some street lights and some buildings that gave off enough light that I could see the surroundings outside a little better.

 Sadly, I could not see the moon from where I was sitting in the small car, but I knew it was still watching over me, I just knew. Suddenly, as she continued to drive out of the neighborhood, I started to recognize where we were. My mind was yelling, "Let me out right here, let me out!" but no words escaped my lips. I guess because I was speaking for so long to God in my mind, I momentarily forgot how to use my voice. I knew in order to survive I had to, I didn't want to keep driving to another place I didn't know, I was done. "Stop, let me out." I said, softly. I couldn't believe the words came out so calmly, so clearly. "Stop the car." I said again. The woman at first said "I can't just stop here, what do you mean?" I repeated, a bit louder, "Stop the car and let me out". The woman pulled into a small hotel on the corner. I recognized it, though usually not a great place to be, especially at night because of the area it was in, but at least I knew where I was and it was good enough for me and better than where I had been earlier. The woman put the car in park and she and the man opened their doors so that Shari and I could get out. I didn't move for a moment, but rather looked at both open doors of the car realizing I wasn't going to be trapped in the small car any longer - not trapped at all. The doors started looking like they were wings and I connected them to freedom. I wept a little inside even though I was still unsure of what was to come next.

THE AFTERMATH

Never regret anything that has happened in your life. It cannot be changed, undone or forgotten. So take it as a lesson learned and move on.

- Author Unknown

I put my foot down onto the concrete driveway of the corner hotel, stepped out, took a deep breath in and let out a huge sigh. The man looked into my eyes as I brushed by him without a word. No one said anything. I walked away from the car not turning back and walked directly into the hotel lobby/24hr restaurant, not even sure if Shari was with me. I didn't look back to see if the small car was still there, I didn't care. I never saw the woman that scared those men away, that drove me out of that neighborhood ever again.

Much later I remember telling my dad about her, without telling him in what condition she found me of course, and asking him if maybe I should try and find out who she was to thank her. I mean, who knows how my life would have turned out if I was left there or if I'd even have a life after that night. He of course disagreed, but I understood since he didn't know the depth of what I went through and what she really did to save me from further torture. I left it alone though I did think of her every so often.

Out of nowhere, I began wondering what I looked like. *Was I dirty? I must have been dirty. I'm sure my back had dirt from laying on that wood by the canal. Was my hair a mess? It had to be. What was I even wearing? Did I ever get my panties back? I wonder what my face looks like.* I felt like I forgot what I looked like, who I was.
Stupid questions that made no sense flipped around my head as the doors opened and the little bit of people that were there turned to look at me. I wonder what they saw. I saw and recognized, as crazy as it sounds, a police officer, a male police officer sitting at a table. I could hardly believe my own eyes - a police officer. I guess because of the area this hotel was in and the fact that it felt really late at night, maybe even early morning, perhaps he was taking a break. I didn't know or care why really, just more crazy thoughts going through my head. Oddly enough, for a moment, I felt a bit safe. A lit-

tle feeling of relief went through me. I wanted to collapse onto the cold floor, or in his arms maybe. I wanted to break down and sob, scream at the top of my lungs. I wanted to pass out. My mind began to clear a little and I began thinking this night may actually be over, praying that it was. The pain inside my body had stopped for a moment. I was not trapped any longer, I wasn't in the car or in the dark, dark night. The bad guys were gone, at least for now, I thought. Maybe, just maybe, I was safe even though they were close enough to come back and shoot me. But for right now, just for that moment, I felt free and like I could breathe a little. However that moment ended quickly and that feeling of okay vanished. I began to feel anxious as I was unsure what was to come next.

I was dating my brother's friend still, though we were technically broken up when this night happened, but we were always breaking up and getting back together at that point. I was 17 years old when this happened. He was never really compassionate about what happened to me, but not many were. It's not their fault, of course, they couldn't understand. I mean, I could hardly believe it happened, and I rarely shared the hurt I felt. I also had no idea how he found out. I believe his step-sister told him, but like anyone that knew, it was, "did you hear Pam got raped?" I believe when he and I did speak about it, I mostly only told him, like many others, only some of what happened. In fact, at that time I was embarrassed to tell anyone, or maybe I just couldn't get those awful words to describe that night out of my mind and into my mouth, if that makes sense. So I always answered his questions with quick simple answers, nothing descriptive.

While dating my ex and dealing with our shit, trying to keep up in high school, partying a little harder with cocaine, weed and anything else that was available, working a part-time job in an office after school, I thought I was living my life like all others. Perhaps I was until that one night my so called 'normal life' became so different and my life seemed to change forever. That misfit girl, that—never tried to fit in, the young Italian girl that loved her big family and enjoyed being around them, the teenager who was just having a good time, everything changed for her that one night.

Kidnapped at gunpoint and raped, again and again, for so many hours, I have no idea how long I was gone that night, but it felt like forever. That certainly can change a person, and it certainly changed me in ways I wouldn't understand until later. Maybe I became more of a misfit. Maybe I was more different than the other friends around me. I felt ugly, strange and unsure for a long time. I'm alive, that I knew, but not yet living. Not yet, not for a long time to come.

When we went up to the officer sitting in the 24- hour restaurant that night in Pompano, I couldn't collapse in his arms like I felt I wanted to. Instead, with tears coming down slowly and looking like somebody beat me up, because in many ways they had, I walked over to the officer and told him that we were raped as I pointed to Shari, who I realized was standing, now, by my side. I could hardly get the words *I was raped* out of my mouth, but I knew I had to. He could tell that something was obviously very wrong because of the tears and how disheveled I must have looked. As I looked down at myself, I saw just how messy I really was. My clothes were all crooked, my hair was a mess, and my face must have looked worn with both the dried and fresh tears. My body ached all over, the events of the night finally hitting me with full force.

It felt like I was bothering him a little, like I was disturbing his break time. I felt a coldness, a discomfort coming from him and decided I couldn't cry, couldn't collapse. So instead, I asked him to please get me home. I believe Shari spoke with him more as we walked outside to his police car. He kept asking basic questions, but I don't remember what they were. I mainly remember Shari speaking for us in the restaurant and once we were in the car. Although I knew I was there physically, my mind was elsewhere. I saw a few people in the restaurant, maybe a waitress, and wondered what they thought of us. I felt so gross, so sick. We walked outside and got into the back of the officer's car and the feeling of being lost, unsure, not safe and trapped crept in again. I just wanted to get home and be with the familiar faces of my family.

As the cop drove towards my house, which wasn't too far away, my thoughts ran wild. When we turned onto my street, my stomach started to hurt. I knew it was late and realized I no longer had my dad's car. The officer told me, "I need you to go in the house, wake up your parents and let them know what happened. I'll be out here waiting." I froze. I couldn't believe what he had just said. Not only was I *still* trying to process what had happened to me, but now this cop, with his cold and, what he thought, simple request, made me want to scream and scratch him in the face. I had no idea how to do what he asked. What would I say? *Hey Mom and Dad, wake up. I was raped tonight, all night and at gunpoint too! Oh yeah, and Dad, they stole your car. Yeah, I said "they". I'm really sorry. Oh and one more thing. I'll need you to hurry it up because there's a police officer out front who wants to speak to you.* How the hell do I do that?! How could he ask me to?

I have been stuck on this part of my story for a while. I thought I was procrastinating, puttin' it off, maybe not sure how to put it into words. But I eventually realized I was afraid to write this part. I was afraid to tell this part of my story, to remember the feelings and to put it on paper. Telling my parents was just as hard, if not harder than what I endured that night. Hurting the ones we love, for me, is a much worse pain. I had woken up my parents many times as a teenager for all sorts of reasons: mostly from coming home drunk or high, calling to say I'm not coming home, I need a ride. Or even once, when my cousins, my friends and I got in trouble with the police, I called them when we nearly got arrested. Those calls were not easy. But waking them now, for this,
telling my parents this, yeah, this will be the most painful. It felt like it wasn't about me any

more, but about them - their hurt, their disrupted sleep, their worry.

I slowly and without a word to the officer, opened the car door. With aches and pains already starting in my body, I walked towards the front door of my house, feeling really sick to my stomach. I thought for sure I was going to vomit or pass out. Jesus, I just wanted to go lie down in my bed, lock my bedroom door and be left the hell alone to try and forget that entire night. But you don't always get what you want because reality gets in the way.

It was dark and quiet when I walked into the house. I could see my parents' bedroom door was closed. They always slept with the door closed because us teenagers were coming in and out all night and because my dad snored like an engine of a Harley Davidson with loud exhaust pipes. I stood at their door, my hand carefully on the knob as I opened it. Their bedroom was so dark but I could make out their bodies, asleep, on the bed. I could hear my dad's snoring. I loved my dad's snoring. It never bothered me growing up, maybe because my room was on the other side of the house and I never heard his rumble. I wondered now, as I stared at them both, how it never bothered my mom. She was so close to that loud engine. My dad was closest to the side of their bed that I was standing over so I put my hand on his shoulder and softly whispered, "Dad." While in my head I was absolutely screaming........ HELP! I felt so sorry for my parents right then. I was almost hoping they wouldn't want to wake up. What I wanted to do was kiss them both good night and then go outside and scream at the top of my lungs. I wanted to tell that officer that I need time to do this. *I'm hurt, I need to breathe, I need a hug, I need help. This is not an easy task. How dare you ask me to do this. Get the hell away from here! Leave just leave!*

Damn reality set in again, and I knew I had no choice. Obviously I could not ask him to leave, and remembered he's still waiting outside for me, but also Shari. We did ask him for help, though at that point I almost regretted it. I was scared, I was taking too long and he may come knocking at our door, so I shook my father again, harder and a little louder this time so he could hear me, "Dad! Dad!" My mom woke up first. *Damnit.* Her head popped up and immediately asked, "what's the matter?" which then caused my dad to wake up. I felt dread wash over my entire body, an absolute sickening feeling in my gut. I wanted to tell them, *nothing sorry, go back to sleep*. But life didn't allow that.

"Dad, I'm so sorry. Dad, there's a policeman waiting outside. You have to get dressed and come outside with me." I couldn't even look at my mom. I tried to not let our eyes meet. "Well, what happened!?" He said in a tone tinged with annoyance, bordering on anger, which I absolutely understood since it wasn't the first time I have woken them when in trouble, but never with a police officer at our door. This, however, was different and I had no idea how it would play out.

He got up quickly and started getting dressed, while my mom continued to ask what was going on. I tried not to answer while still in their bedroom, though I don't know why. I mean, I knew she'd find out eventually, but that's how I did it. I think I was too scared to hurt both of them at once. I'm pretty sure I didn't want to say I had been raped to both of them at the same time, I mean it was going to be hard enough to say it out loud to anyone thereafter. My dad finished throwing on his shorts and shirt and we walked out of the bedroom - my mom remained in the bed, thank God.

As he and I made our way through the living room to the front door, I said it before he could open it, "Dad. Dad, I was raped." I couldn't believe the words had come out of my mouth, that I was actually referring to myself.

It felt incredibly unreal standing in my home while just an hour ago I was actually being raped. I don't remember his response and probably that's best. I'm not even sure he had one.

My dad stood next to the cop as they spoke for a little bit, but I wasn't listening. I didn't want to hear. I didn't care, I guess - maybe I should have, but I didn't. I just wanted to crawl up and disappear, preferably in my bed. After a few minutes my dad turned and looked at me with what looked like confusion on his face. His eyebrows scrunched up, the wrinkles on his forehead more defined and asked if I was hurt. *HURT?!* I mean how in the hell do I answer that?! My God I could barely breathe, never mind speak. My mind was talking again. I was frozen. Did he mean hurt physically? Yes, he must have because how could he know the hurt inside of my head, my body? I mean he couldn't see that pain so he must have meant physically.

"Yes." I said. "I'm hurt." I turned around and lifted up my shirt so he could see my back. I felt pain there, a numbing, sore kind of pain, but I wasn't sure why. So I slowly turned around with my back to him and the officer, still holding up my shirt, not knowing, if anything, was on my back. As soon as I did, I knew it must have been bad based on my father's immediate reaction. He let out a strange sound, something between a yell and painful cry. "Oh Jesus! My God! My God!" He didn't know what else to say or do in that moment, the sounds just came out of him, I certainly didn't blame him, he had no control. I suppose we were both in this very bad dream together now. *I'm so sorry Dad and Mom that I brought you into my reality. What was I thinking?* Honestly, I just wanted to go to bed. I didn't ask what they saw one my back then, but I later learned from photos, and obviously the intense pain that followed, that most of my back had been badly banged up and bruised and that there was some bleeding, most likely from the wood and metal from that night of hell. I knew it would all heal eventually, but would my poor Dad? Would he ever be able to forget that moment?

Before I knew it, I was riding in a car with my mom. I wasn't sure where to at the time, I was just too tired to care or think about it. I guess the police officer made it clear to my parents that I was to immediately go to the clinic so that they could get fingerprints, semen, anything else that may have been left on my body for evidence. My mom must have grabbed some clean clothes for me, assuming they would keep the ones I had on, and we followed the officer in our car. We had no idea where exactly we were going, just that it was a rape clinic and we needed to go.

So there we were, my mom and I, silently driving to a rape center somewhere in the middle of the night, unsure where, just following the behind the officer. I thought the officer took Shari home and we all followed together to the clinic but honestly that part is not really clear. I hardly remember Shari around that night though I assume she was. I don't remember her at the clinic, I don't remember seeing her after the police car pulled into my driveway that night, I actually don't ever, to this day remember seeing her again, crazy. Anyways, I believe the officer went into the clinic first, walked up to the window, said something to the woman there then walked back over to us. Not sure what he said but he left shortly after. I don't remember ever seeing him again either. I do remember sitting in an older, dingy, cold waiting room with my mom, not speaking. I mean what would there be to say? A few moments later they called my name and asked me to follow them to the back. I did - alone.

The examination room was white, cold and dingy. For some reason I remember a lot of what looked like cold metal, like shiny chrome stuff against all white. I remember sitting at the end of the table my feet dangling and my entire body shivering cold. My mind soon started going back to the same place I had been while being raped. I felt nothing but the cool temperature in the room and turned back into a zombie, then like a robot as they gave me directions and I followed. "Remove all your clothes, we'll need them for evidence. Put this paper gown on, lay back on the table with your feet in the stirrups we'll need to do an exam." They spoke in what I interpreted as a deep, robotic mechanical voice, not like women at all. I didn't hear the words clearly, I just knew what they were saying as I felt a hand on me guiding me to lay back on the ice cold table for the examination to gather, I assumed, evidence, proof of what I claimed happened, I guess. They asked a lot of questions that were hard to answer and difficult to explain. The cold hard metal of the exam table and the rough poking around they were doing made it almost impossible for me to think, never mind to answer the questions. No, this was not a date rape. No, not a relative or boyfriend. No, not just one man raped me. I felt they already had the answers to most of these questions from the officer, but were testing me to see if my story matched up to what I told the officer. Little did I know I would be tested over and over again for a long time to follow.

Alone again and staring at the off-white colored ceiling, my mind screamed. *Where's my mom? Why isn't she in here with me so I know someone at least, so I feel a little safe, instead of with all these strangers here in white, in this cold, white room? Why are they so stern and unkind? I want to go home to my room. I want to go to bed, please make them stop. Why is this room so white? Why can't I have a blanket? I'm so cold, these people are so cold. Mom, where are you?*

When the rape happened, I was 17, about to be 18. I was supposed to be going to summer school so that I could graduate that year. I was already behind in all my classes from partying and now I had to deal with the rape and all that would come after. It became too much. I was also working for a builder then and the aftermath of this night affected my job too. As you can imagine, it affected many aspects of my life.

All along I was trying to hide what had happened from everyone so that I could continue my life as best I could, as if nothing bad had happened. Obviously, that was easier to say than do. I was torn up internally, but sometimes that made it easier for me to hide it. Bruises are always easier to see, internal struggles are invisible to those around us. Besides, the ones that knew what happened never asked and the ones that didn't said nothing one way or another. I'm pretty sure no one in school knew, and as far as my "friends", I know some knew, but I was never sure which ones, because they didn't ask, either. However, when mail from the courts or detectives kept coming to my home, my job, or sometimes my school, it got a little harder to hide, but I seemed to pull it off pretty well.

I became good at convincing myself I was okay, thinking I could handle anything on my own. It was pretty easy, in fact, dealing with it on my own, considering no one really asked; I had no choice, no family, no friends I felt I could confide in. It wasn't ever really talked about in my house unless it was forced in our face - like a court date, a detective or police officer knocking at our door. I did not have one person sit with me and ask me about what happened. Not one, not then or ever, to this day. The few people that knew what happened had basic responses like "OMG!" or "Glad you're okay." They only knew I was raped but nothing more - they never asked more. No one knew all the details, because I believe no one really cared enough to ask in a sincere way. The police officers asked plenty of questions, but not with the caring concern I needed. No one ever asked in order to show they cared or to offer help. No one asked.

The only time I can remember feeling ok and like someone actually cared was one night, days after the incident, my dad, my sweet loving dad, came into my room. He sat on the edge of my bed and looked at me. I'm pretty sure he was super uncomfortable, but said some really kind, caring, beautiful things to me in his own way to try and make me feel safe. I remember one thing specifically he said that made me feel safe, "You're safe now, honey. I'm so sure you could go back and walk those streets naked and no one would ever touch you again. I promise you that." You may not think that sounded very comforting, and at the time it may not have been to me, but I knew my dad and how he meant it, so it was nice. Through all this cold ugliness, it was really nice to hear something so sincere come from someone. Of course, it was a little sad it had to be from him, for he shouldn't have to deal with this, but it did make me feel good, safe, yes, maybe a bit comforted for that moment at least, so thanks Dad.

After the night was over and my mom took me home, I believe by then it was early morning. I went into my room and finally got to lie down in my bed, which never felt so good and right. I felt so safe, felt like a baby in a crib. I never wanted to leave. I snuggled up in a fetal position under my blanket and wept into my pillow for hours until I fell asleep, eventually from sheer exhaustion. I cried a lot after that night, alone mostly in my room, it was part of how I hid my pain - alone trying to handle it by myself not letting others see my hurt. I remember waking up on and off throughout the night feeling more and more of the aches and pains in my body and from flashback-like dreams. I remember seeing my dad some of those times I woke, just standing by my bed looking down at me; poor dad, he couldn't sleep either. I was hoping it was all a bad nightmare, but the next morning when I woke, the hurt and pain in my physical body was way worse. Everything hurt. It was similar to pain after being in a car accident, the pain was always worse the next day. I knew it was real, and dammit, I knew I had to deal with it, though I just really wanted to stay asleep to avoid it all, whatever was to come.

I believe no one really asked or spoke much to me, like I said earlier, because from what I do remember I just went on with my life as normally as I could. I tried to make it as normal as possible, and honestly, it wasn't that hard at times. I came and went from my parents house, still went out with my friends, just living my life. Many, many years later I learned that Shari unfortunately made some bad choices and ended up on some heavy drugs and got arrested a lot. I reached out to her once when Facebook came around to see if she wanted to maybe speak of that night, just to see what her memories might be compared to what I remember. I even mentioned maybe writing about it someday - that didn't go well. Let's just say drugs were in her way of thinking. Sad, because we were young and her choices could have been better. The path she chose only led to more heartache. I sometimes wish she would have reached out to me, maybe we could have been there for each other. The very rare time I did see Shari back then after the incident, I tried to ask her how she was handling herself, but some people choose to not speak of their pain and I, of course, respected that then. Not sure how I would handle that today. I might have asked her again.

    The craziness and stress was catching up and affecting my life so I went to work until I got fired because I started partying a little harder which led to missing more work and I stayed in school a little longer until I just quit from the simple craziness of it all. I was so behind in classes already, partying still and dealing with my rape and all that came with it. I made many negative choices that I didn't see as negative at that time.

My ex came around again and over the next few years after the rape, we hardly, if ever, spoke about it. I had dealt with the courts for a long while, always contacting me asking over and over what had happened that night, like maybe I'd tell a different story, but I believe mostly they asked to try and make an arrest. I once was called into a line up, but that was a total waste of time and I felt like they knew it; but, I went along with it a few times, but never recognized any of the men. After what seemed like a year had passed and the courts stopped coming around and I quit dealing with them, he and I remained in the same up and down relationship and eventually married. Over the next few years I had my family of 5, stayed married for close to 20 years (though together longer), and finally divorced in 1999. I sometimes question, how after everything I survived, why I would go and marry into such a tough relationship.

STARTING OVER

Start over, my darling. Be brave enough to find the life you want and courageous enough to chase it. Then start over and love yourself the way you were always meant to.

- Madalyn Beck

I questioned that for a long time. Was this relationship better than or easier to survive than the night of my rape? Was this relationship I walked right back into just comfortable for me, something I was use to and with someone I knew wouldn't bring up my rape? Was our love so strong I could keep pretending? I didn't see these kinds of relationships growing up so how did I allow it and why the hell would I after the way I was treated the night I was raped? Why would I go back and marry this man after our dating issues? Was our love so much better than the way I was now feeling? If only these questions came to me then, or if I had the proper counseling to get some answers, maybe my choices would have been different. But, I didn't and so I learned as I lived, like most of us.

Life went on and I started my own adult journey. Though I continued to pretend my rape wasn't part of my life or who I was, it was pretty simple to do considering it wasn't spoke of. I suffered in silence, within myself. At times I broke down, or had a flashback, a memory, maybe a dream or some issues with something in life that reminded me of that night. But eventually it became easier and easier to pretend to forget, or maybe not pretend, but push it out of my mind. I started making my own decisions and slowly taking my life back. My ex, for a long time during and after our divorce, gave me the hardest time and I felt like my strength was being tested. He'd continue to scare and follow me around, pop up at friend's homes and even a few times, in my home. He threatened me and my family over and over and a few times he threatened suicide. It was very hard and very sad for all of us. I just decided enough was enough and for the sake of myself, my kids and, even for his sake, I had to get a restraining order, which the judge gave me a lifetime one. Over time he broke that order more than once and eventually decided to move away, back to his hometown, up north.

I ask myself today, *why did I live through that? Who was I then?* I have asked myself these questions and so have others asked of me. I loved him through it all, I even understood after awhile why he reacted the way he did. I mean after 25 plus years together it wasn't easy for him either to just start over, but I knew it had to end for all of us and eventually it did. Once he moved away things began to fall into place for the both of us, for all of us because as much as it doesn't feel like it at the time, there is life after divorce, there is life after any tragedy and change does bring change and for the better, most times. I believe it did get better for both him and I, and honestly I believe for our children too. I believe we all got out at the right time, without even knowing it.

During my divorce I had to rely on my dad for help the first year. I'm more blessed than many and I knew it then. I wasn't ashamed that I needed his help, though I knew some thought I should be. I think some people believe they are stronger because they did it all on their own, but I knew I was strong for my own reasons and never felt I needed to prove or justify that to anyone. Maybe I was seen as not a strong, independent woman like some, because, well I needed his help at times and, for the sake of my kids, I asked for it.

Throughout my marriage, I was mostly a stay-at-home mom and honestly pretty tired of being strong, probably some of the reason why today I live the way I do. My parents helped with my mortgage for close to a year and I did the rest, figured it out, got us on food stamps for a while, got two shitty jobs, borrowed and paid back where I needed to. I didn't have many work skills since I was a stay-at-home mom and didn't graduate from high school because, well, life got in my way; but I always worked odd jobs, usually nights after my husband was home. He mostly had the career type, better paying jobs. During the separation I brushed up on my telemarketing sales skills until I got into better positions and into more of an office work environment. It was a struggle, mostly because I felt like I wasn't there for my kids. They were teenagers then and I felt like I was losing them. I worked while they went to school, we were all dealing with the divorce and it sucked, I'm not gonna lie, but it also, at times, started feeling ok because I had my family, my kids. My ex hardly helped at all as far as money, but he too did what he could and I didn't really care so much. After a year I had a job that I settled into that paid the bills. I asked and eventually, through the courts, started getting some child support that I needed. I wanted to keep the peace, so I dealt with whatever I was given - any help was ok.

After the first year and a half, while getting close to my actual divorce, my ex's sister was also going through a bad time with her husband. She and I spoke for a short while during my separation with her brother and she shared with me her marriage troubles - very different than mine but serious because her husband had moved out at the time. Obviously, I knew them both very well and thought I was close with her until she found out not only was I divorcing her brother, but I also had him arrested for breaking the restraining order, twice. When she found out her brother moved back to be near his family, which was near her, we spoke even less. Eventually all contact between his family and I stopped.

One day out of the blue his sister's husband called me. It was sad because I was extremely close to his mom and sister so I was hurt that she couldn't find the words to ever speak to me again. What exactly did I do? I had written his mom a kind letter then, trying to explain exactly what was happening. But to this day I have not received a response and have come to terms with that. I decided it was her choice, her son, her loss, but felt it was unfair to our children, her grandchildren. I believe she and my ex thought the kids should stay in contact with her, but they were going through enough and they were just kids. She was always a good grandmother, but I just didn't understand why a card couldn't be sent to them over the years or a phone call every now and then. But, some things in life we just won't understand.

Eventually, many years later, she did start sending cards again, so I just chalked it up as a hard time for all of us. The last few times I spoke with his sister I was told that I could speak to her, just not about her brother, which seemed odd to me at the time, but I just agreed because, again, I just wanted peace. She and her husband were still going through their own rough time, not anything abusive, just a different difficult time like I said. I remember being in that family and her husband always being kind to everyone; however, I was surprised when I received that call out of the blue from him to see how I was doing. His call came after the last night my husband and I were together, after he was arrested for breaking the restraining order. He said he heard from his wife that I was going through a rough time and going through a divorce and was just checking on me to see if I was ok. He also told me that he had paid to bail out my ex since it was his wife's brother after all. I thought that was kind, it really didn't matter to me. I just couldn't believe he even cared enough to check on me, his kindness overwhelmed me, it made me cry, I certainly wasn't used to it. I just couldn't believe, through all the ugliness someone reached out, someone sincerely asked if I was ok. It wasn't about my rape, obviously, because he didn't know, but it was about a really tough time I was going through. So I thanked him and left it at that.

We spoke again for a short time months later - he was going through his own marital problems still which became worse as time went on, and my divorce was coming to an end. He talked and I listened mostly then. I always recognized that he and I were not like the families we married into. I realized there was an attraction, something I felt was always there because of who he was but I had not thought about it until I started talking to him more one on one and while divorcing. It wasn't a sexual attraction at first but a very strong attraction to each other's personalities or, maybe, the things we both believed in. The way we felt about things in general like our kids, music, sex, politics, family, whatever it was we just seemed to click, it felt easy, nice like how it should be, something that neither one of us had in our marriages spouses that really listened. I guess we didn't listen to each other back then.

We mostly stayed away from talking about our exes in the beginning, or soon to be exes, and just kept it simple and light. He had moved out of his home then and was considering divorce. I suggested to him, since they never had, to at least try a marriage counselor, if not for them, for their kids. They did, but during just one visit, the first, and what would be the only visit, he found out some information which caused him to soon after file for divorce. He was devastated, as divorce for some is like a death, and he truly loved his wife at the time so this hurt him deeply. I became divorced within a year and he was still in the midst of becoming divorced. We kind of supported each other mentally throughout over the phone since we lived over 1200 miles apart, plus the fact I was no longer allowed to speak to anyone on my ex's side, so I decided to do what was best for me. Our calls over the years became more personal, more about feelings, life, children. Eventually, the calls became more serious, more deep, way more intimate. Once he was near his final months of divorce and I already was, I invited him to come visit. I needed to see what this was and why I was feeling so strongly about him. What was that original attraction I felt so long ago? I needed to know because it wasn't going away; it seemed to be growing stronger and it's crazy that we were both in this position. There was always something about him and the only reason I'm sharing this in my story, is so others can know, not only can you go through years of struggles and ugliness, of pain and sorrow, but you can come out finding a love and happiness that is beyond what you could have ever imagined, and it comes once you set yourself free to see all your opportunities, your choices not the ones set by the rest of the world.

Throughout both our marriages and all the family events that we'd see each other at, there was something, an electricity I couldn't explain and didn't try to at that point. I just ignored it, though I did speak about it to a few friends because it was unfamiliar and yet felt strangely good. I can remember the first time seeing him. My ex wanted me to meet his family up north since I knew all his family in Florida already. His stepdad at the time offered to fly down and fly me back with him for Christmas to surprise my ex, like I was going to be his gift for the holidays. I remember that visit so clearly. It was such a strange time in my life for a few reasons. Strange because I was excited at the thought of seeing my boyfriend after so many months, I missed him. Plus I'd be meeting his family for the first time, but also strange because it would be the first time I was hit by that man I thought would love me forever and never hurt me, especially physically. Yet also beautifully strange because I first was introduced to a man there I had no idea I'd lock eyes with and feel such electricity that I'd eventually be with for the rest of my life, true love at first sight - yes it does happen.

It was Christmas then and snowing and freezing in the north and silly me had a cute Christmas like dress on, with stockings so yeah that kind of helped. His step-dad first took me over to meet his mom at her home, dropped off my luggage and visited for a bit but they both knew how anxious I was to see their son so his step-dad took me to his sister's house where my ex was with his friends and some family. I was nervous but more excited just to see my boyfriend and be in his arms. I walked in and first met his sister. She was beautiful and looked a little like her brother, and I was happy to meet her. She was cooking in the kitchen, we only chatted for a short time because I was excited to surprise her brother. She told me they were all in the basement playing pool. As I walked through the kitchen and down the basement stairs to surprise my ex with his gift, *me*, I got halfway down and realized there were quite a few people there. My eyes glanced around looking for my boyfriend but only one man, who I had no idea at the time who he was, stood out. I realized quickly it wasn't my ex and that this stranger and I were both locked onto each other's eyes and frozen right there in time, right there while I was still halfway on the staircase. I'm sure others noticed but hoped not. "OMG" I heard a man's voice yell. I looked away from this stranger and saw my then boyfriend (my ex-husband) coming towards me with his arms wide open. We hugged and I was happy but *never* forgot that moment with the stranger, never forgot what a strong, yet odd feeling that was. Who would have guessed that he would later become my brother-in-law and much later in life my husband, my life.

We lived 1200 miles apart at the time and both were married, so over the years I chose to not think of him much, though I knew the feeling was always there, something I couldn't pretend happened that day. The times I did see him over the many years we were married at family functions, we later learned others felt our attraction too.

During our divorces I went on a few dates and I'd share some of my date stories with him over the phone and he would share his. But eventually, when we realized there may be something between us, those date stories felt uncomfortable to hear. Suddenly it didn't matter to me that we were once family by marriage because now, we were just single people on this earth - our marriages ending and new lives beginning. We were friends and it felt amazing and we both deserved this chance. Though it did matter to me what our kids would think since they were all cousins and always would be. It mattered but I couldn't allow it to sway my choices then.

After really considering everything and even knowing what others would think, I chose to make my own decisions and start living for me. I felt like I was slowly taking part of myself back, with every decision I made and doing what I thought was right for myself and my family, though they could not see at the time. In the past, for the longest time, I felt like I wasn't allowed to do what I wanted because I always had someone over me, judging me, making fun of me, talking about me, belittling me and putting me down: bullies, abusers, just mean people. I listened to what everyone else thought I should do and never to myself. I worried too much and for too long about what the world thought and how things were supposed to go, what you should or should not do based on society. Like marrying because you're pregnant or going to marriage counseling while being abused at home. That is all bullshit to me now. So with both of us free from marriages, though I knew it would be difficult and knew most wouldn't understand, I needed and wanted to see him so we could talk in person. I could no longer make my life choices based on who would understand or not. If I could survive all I had, people could find ways to understand my choices, or not, and that would be their choice. So I asked him to come visit, and he immediately said yes and flew down the next month. We drove directly to the ocean from the airport and sat on a beach talking for hours and hours, face to face, eye to eye, calmly, slowly, both listening as the other spoke. We even spoke about the first time we saw each other that day on the stairs. Crazily enough he told me almost the exact same story, he said he too felt something unfamiliar and good that day we locked eyes. We continued talking, really taking the time to hear what the other was saying, like it mattered. Something neither of us were used to in our first marriages. I couldn't believe he was sitting in front of me. It was almost like a beautiful scene in a romantic movie. I never felt so attracted to someone's smile, words and laughter. I felt so safe. It wasn't weird that he was once married to my husband's sister, because I always saw him simply as a kind man, and at that time we were just two people walking this earth alone. I knew the road ahead would be scary, and it was for a while. We were tested not only by life, but by our exes who decided they would try to persuade our kids and some family to hate us and speak made up awful rumors about us, while only doing so to deflect from their own wrong doings. He and I stood together knowing it was their own hurt and guilt at play, so we didn't speak ill of them, just allowed everyone to believe what they chose at the time, kept our truths and let time reveal all.

We hoped that in the end our friends and kids would see the truth, like all things in my life, I knew it was in God's hands. I also knew this electricity I felt was real, yet unexplainable. I refused to defend it to anyone that questioned it. I ignored the ridiculous lies that were being spread and watched, as time went on, the truth came out and the beauty of our relationship bloomed. We agreed to stand strong together and live by our truths and just let life take us where it would. And boy did it.

We dated long distance for over a year and he eventually moved in, though he definitely visited in between. We lived together through some really difficult times due to others, but mostly had amazing, fun, adventurous times. After seven years of living together we eventually married in 2007 and I still, today, feel safe and loved with him. He's someone that asks and listens to my answers and then asks what I need - we do this for each other. After all the crap I've been through, the hardest part was listening to what everyone else thought I should do. This man allows me to be myself and loves me for that. Once I stood up and made my own decisions, my own mind, my own choices, my life fell beautifully into place; it started to flow. I believe today this man knows me like no other. He is by far the most supportive person in my life and it's so refreshing to be able to not only trust him but to trust each other, and that's big for us. He's not only been supportive and understanding about my past, but for just about anything. We support each other because we believe in each other.

The life we live looks different to others, but he and I know why we make the decisions we do and love the way we live, and that's all that matters. We are free in this relationship to live as we feel and have no need to ever explain ourselves to anyone. If you love us you just know the truth and eventually our kids saw that truth, they see how we live, our love and our truths. It's never easy to know one of your parents caused a breakup, but our kids know we once loved their parents but this is today and with life, comes changes. Choosing each other was one of the best choices we made and we only wish we had more time together, since marrying so late in life, but it happened as it should as everything else always does.

Like a lot of choices I had to make, it was also then my choice, after my rape, to stop going to court hearings and dealing with the police, detectives and lawyers that I felt not only didn't care, but didn't help my healing; they only hindered it. It was my choice to leave school when I knew it was affecting me and causing me so much extra stress while trying to get through it and deal with the rape. I suppose it was my choice to not share a lot of what I went through then about my rape or even about the abuse in my marriage. It was my choice to party and do drugs, my choice to marry and have children, my choice to divorce and no longer allow that man, or any other, to ever control me, put hands on me or speak ill to me in any way ever again. It was also my choice to marry again, even knowing so many didn't agree due to our situation - a man once my brother-in-law by marriage, now my husband, makes me so glad I didn't listen to any of them.

I've had enough of following these made-up, bullshit rules of what's right or wrong. What's wrong for you might not be for another. If I had listened to the ridiculous immature thinking of others, I may have lost one of the best humans and loves of my life. I've made both good and bad choices over the years like anybody else. Today it is my choice, though I know many may be affected by my story, to write something I believe needed to be said in the way I thought it should be said. The truth has always been the only way and my husband and I always stuck to that truth. It really will set you free!

YOU'RE NOT ALONE

To anyone who is struggling today, you are enough. Your feelings are valid. You matter to someone.

- Dau Voire

I survived. You survived. We survived. Each abused differently but hurt the same. Evil, sick humans that tried to destroy us but instead only took advantage of who we were at the time. Some weak, some innocent, some children, some adults. They did some damage, true, but this gave some of us ammunition, weapons of knowledge, to fight back with unexplainable strength! I refused, as weak as I was then, I refused to allow that night from my past to affect who I was to become.

In many ways I chose to remember what I survived so when speaking my mind or making a choice it brings up my strengths. I did not allow my past to make me hateful. Being raped as I was, did not stop me from having healthy, loving, good relationships or accepting or giving love. It did not give me fear whenever I was alone or in dark nights or driving in a car. I would not allow it to take away any of my joy or my belief in God. Man can be cold and ugly at times, this I knew for sure, but never did I allow that knowledge to turn to hate. For I also knew there were so many good humans in this life too, and there still are. It's my choice to always see the good in people first. Some have definitely hurt me and changed me in many ways, but never did they destroy me completely. That would mean they killed me and dammit, I'm alive for a reason! I wasn't going to let that happen. I stayed alive well after so I could have that family of my own through good and bad. I loved my husband at the time and we raised those kids with love. I put away my own hurt and pain so they could have a chance at a happy home.

Don't hide abuse, and certainly don't ever accept it, as I did for way too long. I didn't know better, but you do now. Know that one form of abuse is no less than others - verbal, mental or physical. Don't pretend everything is okay when it's not. Don't not talk about it or think you can handle it yourself, you can't, and for God's sake don't believe the abuser is any different from all the other stories you've heard, he's not. Your situation is *NO DIFFERENT* than the millions of others. The love you feel for that person/abuser is the same all victims feel. Yes I said *abuser*, your boyfriend or girlfriend, husband or wife. If the person you love has ever put their hands on you in any hurtful way or tried in any way to control you, they are an abuser. And yes, you will remain a victim until you have woken up, learned and left. You cannot change them. If you really love yourself as much as you believe you love them, you'd set them free to make their own choices, find their own way and get the help they need.

Even if time goes on and they make some changes, if you accept them back, they will get comfortable and slowly the situation will begin reverting back to what it was before and you're once again dealing with the abuse. Take charge and stay in control. You have so much power!

If you don't know what real love feels like and are accepting what you think it is, find out from others that do know. If you see any signs of hurt from the person that is supposed to be loving you, stop feeling bad for them, stop making excuses and thinking you're just arguing like all couples, you're not. Stop believing you can help or change them, you can't, you can't change them, only your own situation. I can't say that enough! It's their past, their damage and they need to seek their own help, as you and I do for any of our own issues. Let them go, pray for them, forgive them, forgive yourself and move on.

If you don't know all the signs from the beginning, ask. This life is yours, you're in control and life goes fast, my friends. So live in the moment and always be yourself. Demand respect and be who you are. It's the only way to find out if you and the other person will survive the relationship, by being your true self. Watch for the little things in the beginning. Let me share a story with you.

I remember listening to some hip-hop music at home when my former husband walked in and just said "why do you listen to this shit? It's not for adults. Aren't you embarrassed?" So I'd sneak and listen to it. Then it was "why don't you wear skirts? You never wear skirts like other girls?" So I started wearing more skirts and dresses to please him. Then it was "isn't that skirt too short? Pull it down. That dress makes you look like a hooker", etc., etc. Eventually it was my hair, my body, then my friends. It once was his gentle hands holding mine, caressing my body, playing with my hair, and in a blink of an eye his hands were smacking me, twisting me, pushing me down and pulling my hair. Then, eventually, instead of gentle kisses there was spit dripping down the center of my face. But better than a punch right? Or so I'd tell myself. Sound familiar? You get where I'm going?

It's the little things. If I knew then what I know today, I may have saved myself and many others from unnecessary hurt. But I didn't, so I'm telling you now. Be yourself 100%, and the right person will love you as you are without asking you to change a thing or make comments to embarrass or degrade you. It will be the opposite, in fact. You will be able to be your beautiful self and have the person that loves you appreciate and respect you for it, trust and honor you. Their hands will remain soft and kind as their kisses will stay beautiful.
True Love is beautiful.

I believe I survived that tragic night and went through my divorce so I could meet my husband today and move forward in a blessed life. We cannot allow any part of our life that was awful or painful to ruin the rest of our years. Instead, we need to learn from it. If you need help learning to do that, reach out and ask for it.

Sometimes I do wonder, if had I gotten therapy back then and not in my late 50s, what would have happened. But then I immediately know it doesn't matter. I am not going to live with "what if's ". I did pretty well, I made it through the best I could, it's what we all do. It did affect my life, obviously, in many ways though I didn't see how until much later. I know that today, for those who are abused, it's most likely, in some ways, affected your life too. But, it's all how you decide to handle it. How you decide to make the rest of your life matter. Again, if you can't do it alone, ask for help.

Am I sorry my kids had to go through some of my shit? Of course! But, like every single one of us, we are just living this ride as best we can. I always tell my kids buckle up, life's a freaking roller coaster of ups and downs, but you chose to stay buckled and safe or fall off into the unknown. People have asked me how I survived, how I stayed the good human I am today and even back then, putting others before me, how I could be with men again, how I wasn't always angry, how I didn't want to kill myself at times. I can't answer those questions, and I'm hoping this book explains some, but some things in life cant be answered so you just move on. Best I can say is, I got through with God, prayer and my own beliefs. We just all have our own survival techniques, I suppose. Giving up just wasn't an option for me. I can tell you my past actually helped me get through a lot of life with my own children as they grew into adults. I have been there when they suffered and have always stayed strong for their sake. I once didn't speak up and today I don't shut up. That's all from living the past life I lived. In tragedies sometimes we can grow stronger, I know I did.

I had a lot of, what I call today, psychic moments. I think it's part of being an empath with a strong instinct. I'm not talking about speaking to the dead, but I am talking about *seeing* things that happened somewhere else as they were happening, getting visits from loved ones, feeling others' energy, be it good or bad. My instincts became stronger as I got older and I eventually learned to use it to help me grow spiritually. I ignored a lot of the occurrences or instincts in my younger years, like the NO I heard before I entered the neighborhood that night. Eventually I learned to use my instincts, always with God's guidance. I know now that all struggles are opportunities to learn from. I found ways through my struggles through prayer, peace and listening to my inner self to not only get by but to become better. I learned to share with others what I had learned with the hope they could use that knowledge to make better choices and find their own peace. It's crazy to me sometimes that I was able to find peace in my life but I know I was able to because I refused to let any of the past affect who I would become. God was my therapist that I relied on daily on my path to peace. On my journey, I became a great pretender - pretending I was okay and doing just fine. It was my natural way of getting through my struggles. It wasn't just until later that I learned I didn't need to pretend but that my truth would set me free.

I always allowed people to do what they did and forgave them, mostly with the understanding that they had gone through times in their life and are who they are. I had come to terms with the fact that no one asked me about that catastrophic night in my life. I always just tried to understand that. But after a while and still sometimes, now, many years later, I think, *Do I? Do I really understand?* I am always the one to make sure others know I'm here for them. I ask them their stories and what they may need because I care. I ask to see if I can help or just be there to listen, maybe even make them smile. So I question sometimes all the people that didn't ask. Did they not care? Was it too uncomfortable for them so they just chose not to ask? I should understand that right? Should I? From the court system that tore me up and tried to make me believe I somehow did this, provoked that night by my need, as they stated, to get high or by the clothes I wore. Should I be understanding of them? Should I understand they think I got what I deserved? I mean they have a lot of cases, they see this all the time, right? Should I understand their reasons, their excuses? How about the employees at the rape clinic where I had a glimpse of hope for some compassion but only received people doing their jobs and treating me cold, like I was a corpse on a slab. Should I understand that? My friends, friends that never asked then. I never asked why they never asked, was it for me to be understanding, to understand their reasons why? Maybe. My family, from my parents to my brothers, cousins, aunts and uncles, did they even know? Even my ex-husband who not only didn't ask or care at the time but decided later to take it upon himself, during our divorce, to tell my kids I was raped, without even knowing the entire story, without ever considering speaking to me first. Should I understand why he did that and why none of them ever asked? Was it nice of me that I said nothing so my kids would think highly of me by not confronting their dad about it? Always considering others, but no consideration for me, it's my story to tell when I felt they and I were all ready to tackle it. But instead he took that from me! For my children, I do understand, they shouldn't have to ask, they didn't have to know then, at least not until I chose to tell them. But, for the others, should I really understand?

I'm not angry. I'm just tired and at times I'm really frustrated that the world doesn't understand me or maybe that I don't understand the freaking world. Though I do try, a lot of times I give up because the world is just too big and confusing, too much to understand. So, I just keep trying to understand myself. One of the things that confuses me at times is why people don't ask. I mean I would ask someone I knew who had been hurt or damaged to tell me their story, just to find out if I could maybe help in some way or be someone to genuinely listen to them. But again, that's just me. A few times I did ask and they got offended and didn't want to talk, so I left it alone, but at least I asked.

I didn't go to funerals for the longest time for my own reasons, but eventually, through a good friend, I learned it wasn't about me or how uncomfortable I may have felt, it was about the families hurting. So I changed my ways and it made me question even more why, if I could see that and care enough to change, why could nobody ask me still even though it may very well be uncomfortable for them. Today I just want all survivors, no matter their tragedy or their story, to know I will ask and there are many people that will ask, that do care enough to offer help, and if you can't find those people that ask you, then you go ask for the help, even if you have to shout it out loud in the middle of a room filled with people so they hear you or on the top of a mountain side out loud to God. Don't ignore it and think *I've got this* like I did for so long. I probably should have asked for help sooner. I sometimes wish I did, but I'm trying to save you from the struggle today. Again, I have no regrets, believe it or not, I'm not sorry that night happened, it taught me that no matter what life hands me I will not be ugly to others of this world. I will not go through life angry, which doesn't mean I haven't been, just that I will always choose to find the moon's light in the dark skies. I don't regret my first marriage either. I was in love and it taught me to be tough, to demand respect from others and to never again allow anyone to treat me anything less than great. My past gave me a strength I never thought I'd be able to have, the girl once teased that said nothing would never allow that today. Always a beautiful misfit, that

I will still claim, but not the same. I am grateful for the life God has given me and I will continue to live it by my choices and my beliefs and can only hope others can see the good in themselves too. I am in NO way trying to make anyone take on my beliefs or even try to understand my choices or beliefs. We all have our own, and I respect that.

My story is to also let others know that I was just a young girl, maybe just like you, where life started out so kind and through all the hard and sometimes unbearable moments we can come out stronger. You cannot only survive but be better and maybe eventually even be proud of the misfit you are.

To all the victims that may be reading this, remove that label and know you are now survivors, soldiers if you will. Shit, you are a rockstars! You were never at fault, nothing you said or did made this happen to you. You didn't have a choice then, but today you can stand up to all of them. The bullies that made fun of you for your different hair or thick body, today you know they are the ones that are insecure and hurting. The ugly adults that were family members scaring you into trusting them, threatening you not to tell or the priests or teachers, bosses, doctors, babysitters, that tricked you into believing in them as they ripped out your innocence, the boyfriends or dates that started out fun until they took from you as they pleased without ever considering its your body not theirs. Those are the real cowards and the ones that are at fault. Kidnappers, rapists, all sick humans and all of them are at fault. Never was it your fault, never was it mine. Nothing I did or wore that night, not the way I acted or the reason for going to get a five dollar bag of weed, did I deserve the suffering I endured from the hands of those men. The best revenge against those people and a great way to be happy is to decide to live your life to the fullest, your way. Make the choices that are best for you.

I chose my husband today even knowing the struggles we would have with others, and it continues to be one of the best choices I ever made. Also tell, don't keep secrets. Turn for help, don't turn to shit like drugs or wait for depression to set in. Don't allow anger to guide your life and never, ever consider suicide because then, the abusers win. And that should never happen, no matter the crime. They took enough from you and they should never be allowed to take more. You're too brave, too strong and alive today for so many reasons. You have too much life to live and love to give. Those criminals will get the lives they deserve eventually, even if you don't get to see it.

Years later, when I was in my late 50's an event in my life that involved my daughter changed me again and for the first time in my life I asked myself for help. I told my husband I couldn't breathe and that I believe I needed some therapy to help me through some stuff and of course he said "ok babe". So I googled therapists near me, I read the bios and saw the faces of many. I used my trustworthy intuitions and had a good feeling about this one female therapist and nervously made the call to book an appointment. Her voicemail came on - thank goodness because I was truly scared - so I left her a message. 24 hours later I got the call, I swear I was starting to talk myself out of it when she called, but I decided I needed to try so I answered. We spoke and days later I walked into her office, where I continued to go for many years to come. All the years I thought "I got it", it turns out I only had some of it. I mean, I couldn't walk across an intersection with eyes upon me until I met with her and had no idea that was from part of my traumatic night. I sat in her office and the first thing I did was put a pillow on my lap and hold it, I didn't know why I did any of this strange stuff until I met her. I learned it was my form of protection, hiding if you will. She was eventually able to help me to not only understand why I did some of those strange things I did, but over time I learned to say with certainty "I got this!" And thanks to her, I learned so much more about myself and continue to do so daily. My strength today didn't come easy and believe me, I'm not always strong, but I'll always survive and get back up. For me this belief came from my dad who I'm sure got it from my grandmother. She definitely instilled in me to always see the good, even in the really bad moments. She gave my dad the same beliefs, though I got that from both my parents. Today, God and my amazing therapist are two of the many reasons my words are finally on paper. For someone like me, who didn't understand, or maybe believe in therapy, my therapist was a true inspiration in so many ways and I can't thank her enough. Thank you, Dr G.

My hope is that anyone struggling today can take from my story that not only can you survive, but with time you can rise above all the hurt and pain. Your mind controls all your thinking and choices, so choose well, choose what's best for you. I can't say it enough.

We survived. You survived. I survived. We are survivors, rock stars, and I pray you all find ways to understand that being different is beautiful and any hurt you have endured can allow you to bloom into someone more powerful and more magnificent. We are not damaged; we have just been hurt. We find our own ways to survive through our own strengths and our own beliefs. We need to continue being not just ok with our misfit labels but find ways to feel proud of them. We know who we are and what we have been through and were ok not fitting into anyone's mold. We are brave beyond what others could ever understand and I for one will always ask you even if I'm uncomfortable, even if the answer is you don't want to share right now, I will come ask again if you're ok, what you need, to tell me your story. I care. Always remember, we are no longer victims, just beautiful misfits, survivors, fighters, strong brave rock stars, really beautiful souls that will carry on if someone asks...or not.

In ending my story, I'd like to tell you today I am happily married still to the love of my life, we live a simple, fun life surrounded by good family and friends. We're always having a good time filled with laughs, trying to make others laugh too, while always being kind. We support each other by listening, talking and respecting each other's needs and yes, he always asks if I'm ok, he asks. We have 7 beautiful children and 9 amazing grandchildren, and I only end my story by telling you all this so you know, whatever it was that hurt you, it can all turn around if you just believe and fight for you.

> *"I love the person I've become, because I fought to become her."*
>
> *-Kaci Diane*

Made in the USA
Columbia, SC
01 March 2022